Blond Boy

Lucia May

Evening Street Press

Dublin, Ohio

Evening Street Press

March 2014

Dublin, Ohio

Acknowledgements

I would like to thank the following for publishing some of the poems from *Blond Boy*, and for their kind permission to reprint them here:

Burnt Bridge: The D-Day Issue: "Blond Boy's German Meals," "Blond Boy at Bischofsheim," "Boys Trading," "Blond Boy at Work in Scotland After the War."

Evening Street Review: "Racist in Training."

Winning Writers War Contest: "Life Expectancy."

The Little Red Tree International Poetry Prize Anthology 2010: "For Any Abiding Place on Earth."

The Awakenings Review: "Unbeknownst to You My Brother."

Photo credits: Author photo and pg. 36, Chelsea May Tischler.
Cover, "Lucian in Scotland After the War," facing pg. 1, "Family Collage," and "Grandmother 'Babcia' Browislawa," — family photo collection.
Kathryn Kuhlmann, — Joan Gieson

ISBN: 978-1-937347-17-8
Printed in the United States of America

www.eveningstreetpress.com

To Karson
the first of the next

and with loving thanks to
Bruce
and our children
Liz, Chelsea, Alex and Ellery,
for their technical, photographic,
and inspirational brilliance

and my sister Kathy,
sister-in-law Jane Coppock,
and my friend
Jane Levin

Grandmother "Babcia" Bronisława

Forgiveness is the answer to the child's dream of a miracle by which what is broken is made whole again, what is soiled is made clean again.

—Dag Hammarskjold

Contents

WAR

A. Butlin Holiday
Picture

Blond Boy

The blond boy runs with his pigeon
at his chest along the border
of "Germany" and occupied Poland.
He is running to his friend's
house to trade pigeons.
The blond boy's father drops his scythe
in the family field as a brown-shirted
Wehrmacht soldier on bended knee
aims his Mauser at the boy and fires.

The blond boy becomes an old man.
He tells this story in a Cleveland diner.
He does not say anything
about Jewish boys' corpses in mass graves
and how they were flattened
by earth and other stacked corpses.
How the corpses were called *figuri*,
which in Polish means *figures*,
not *bodies*. These are not his stories.

His stories are the glories of God's miracles.
Our Lord Jesus in his infinite wisdom
spares him, his humble servant,
to live and spread the Word of His mercy.

Blond Boy and the Plan for Eastern Europe (*Generalplan Ost*)

Cattle wagons transported
children aged six to ten years
to temporary selection camps.
A sympathetic Nazi guard
could sell a Catholic child back
to its Polish family for 25 *złoty*.

The blond boy is twelve in 1939
when the Nazis invade Poland.
He is too old for Germanization,
too old to be desirable enough
to undergo racial exams by experts.

Some younger Polish gentiles live
and die as Germans, unsuspecting,
but he is too old to forget Polish
nursery rhymes and his Polish name.

Armed Nazis seize him from the family farm
and he is conscripted as a *Zivilarbeiter*—
civilian worker— forbidden to swim
in public pools, to ride public transport,
to own a bicycle or, under penalty of death,
to have sex with a German.

By law the blond boy's wages are lower than
German citizens', his nutrition substandard.
He chips stone seven days a week
in a German quarry. He may not attend
church and must wear a purple "P" badge.

His superiors encourage him to sign
the *Deutsche Volksliste* for benefits
like more calories and freedoms.
He refuses to sign and after the war
is spared being tried in Poland for high treason.

Blond Boy and the Weaker Sex

When the boys were seized from their families
by the Germans to dig anti-tank
trenches in the Polish countryside,
they were first sent on cattle cars to Nuremberg.

For three days and three nights
there was no food, water, or heat.
There were no bathrooms in the train cars.

Being a clean people, the Nazis,
upon the boys' arrival, ordered them to strip
and stand in line outside for several cold hours
to await their turn to shower at a single spigot.

The female guards enjoyed gawking
at the boys and fondling them with sticks.
If a boy responded with an erection,
a guard struck it.

The blond boy grew up and marveled
that he and the prisoners did not rebel,
that the boys accepted their penalties
like cows on the farm before the knife.

Blond Boy and the Goat

The blond boy and his fellow workers
hammer rock in a quarry
at the base of a mountain.
Sometimes the boys fight over rats to eat.
Daily the guards send them
up the mountain to the main
prison camp to carry down food.

One day the blond boy and his friend
walk up the mountain where a goat
bleats in a crevice. They wait until night
to skin and butcher it in small pieces
to hide in their clothes. They bury the raw
meat in the ground by the barracks
until they can collect wood
to roast it in secret.

Blond Boy in Bischofsheim, Germany

In January 1945 the blond boy
and four friends found a train
bombed and derailed by the Allies.
They clambered inside the frozen
wreckage and seized slabs
of German smoked bacon rations.
The boys carried the meat
in rucksacks until the end of the war
but never ate it because they would
probably be hungrier tomorrow.

Blond Boy and the Bomb Shelter

The laborers usually stay in the barracks
for bombing raids but one time
the blond boy and his friend sneak out
to the Nazis' bomb shelter.

The "P" for Polish sewn on their jackets
gives them away. The Nazi guards
push them out to crouch
in an open field at the quarry.

When the raid was over the blond boy and his friend
walk back from the field and see only,
where the barracks and shelter had been,
a crater in the ground.

Blond Boy Carries Soup from the Prison Camp

The blond boy and his epileptic friend
decide that the next time they carry
their fellow workers' dinner down
from the prison camp in the mountain,
the blond boy will carry the bucket of soup
and his friend will carry the potatoes.

Boys Trading

Air raid sirens, the unholy opposite of silence,
flood and benumb reason and sensibility.

The teen blond boy exits from an underground
German latrine that doubles as a bomb shelter.

A confused young German soldier accosts him,
hands him his pistol and raises his arms in surrender.

They fall on each other's necks and weep.
The blond boy wants to believe that the German
boy is correct that the war is over.

The blond boy remembers his Polish friend
who traded pigeons with him and the first
German soldier who shot at him at the farm in Poland.

The blond boy soon stops the tearful dance,
slowly hands the gun back to the muddled soldier
and says in broken German,
the war is not yet over.

Terror wins the German boy's face
as he shoves the gun back in its holster
and sprints in the direction of his unit.

The blond boy is glad that the German boy
will probably not be punished
for surrendering his weapon to his enemy.

Blond Boy's German Meals

At the end of the war in Nuremberg
daylight backdrops aerial parades
of Allied bombers and their falling shells.
All people below are deafened into chaos.

The labor camp guards flee for their lives.
Allied lorry drivers round up stray workers
and drive through the Alps towards Italy
where the Second Polish Corps is being trained.

During stops in the German countryside
the blond boy and others newly freed
forage for food in garbage cans
and sometimes find fresh bread inside
wrapped neatly by German farmer wives.

Blond Boy at Work in Scotland After the War

On the first day
the mineshaft elevator cage
drops him 450 feet
between heart beats.

The blond boy weeps
and asks himself
which are worse,
Nazis or coal mines.

He lies on his back
on a dolly with a shovel.
Eighteen inches from his eyes,
the crawl space ceiling
drips its sweat onto his face.

He remembers a Nazi sport:
they'd build two parallel walls
shoulder width apart
and high enough to stand within.

They'd stuff people
in between the walls single file
and build a ceiling
to seal them off to die.

At the end of the shift
kids pass him on bicycles
as he walks home to Mrs. White
who shares her rationed eggs with him
and calls him "son."

MORE CRIMES AND MIRACLES

Kathryn Kuhlmann

Lucia

The former blond boy,
my father, Lucian,
emigrated to the United States in 1951.

He soon married my mother, Helen,
who had two children, Kathy and Billy,
by her first husband.

I was born in 1959
as Lucian was beginning his attempts
at middle American family life.

BURGLAR

Before my parents' first separation I awoke one night to find the police at our house. My parents knew that my brother Billy sneaked out his bedroom window at night to drink beer with his thirteen-year-old buddies. That night they locked his window when he was gone and left the side door open with the lights out. Later when Billy returned he found his bedroom window locked and the basement window grout planted with razor blades. So he sneaked in the kitchen door. My father, who had been waiting in the dark, pushed him down the steep stairs to the basement. My mother called the police and said, "A boy just broke into our house." So the police took him to jail and kept him until the next day when my parents admitted to knowing who he was. For the rest of his life Billy would have the scar where his teeth pierced his lip as he fell.

Don't Forget

My mother separated from my father, Lu, when I was five because there was an incident with my sister. He wanted me to call him on the phone every night. I forgot one evening and when I realized my mistake the next day, I called him in a panic. He told me, "If you really loved me you wouldn't forget." On Saturdays when we had our "dates" he would sometimes draw me cute pictures of cats and squirrels. Sometimes he drew sad pictures of pierced hearts with blood dripping, or an old woman, his mother in Poland. When he'd drop me off at my mom's, I'd run to my bedroom and cry.

After many months my mother let Lu move back in with us. She was afraid that the authorities would find her an unfit mother since Kathy and Billy were getting into trouble. She said she took Lu back because she was afraid the law would take me away since we had an unstable (fatherless) home. My sister, then seventeen, moved out of the house immediately, rented an apartment and started working as a legal secretary.

At age thirteen, my brother Billy began his many stays in homes for juvenile delinquents, the last of which was the infamous Father Gibault's Boys' School, in Terre Haute, Indiana, the purported former home of Charles Manson and, some said, Al Capone.

Billy's violin was now available to me. On a visit home from Father Gibault's, Billy grabbed his violin from me as I was tuning it. In response, Lu broke a dining room chair over Billy's back.

I asked for violin lessons and to my surprise Lu acquiesced. My school was offering violin lessons for five dollars a semester. He was quick to tell me that if I were truly talented, I wouldn't need lessons. "Mozart," he said, "was self taught." I wasn't allowed to say, "Ok." I was required to answer, "Yes, Daddy Dear."

Racist in Training, 1967

I'm seven. My parents and I
are in a Polish tour bus
going to Oświęcim.
The English way to say)
it is Auschwitz.
The tourists on the bus eat
gooseberries and sing
Polish songs and prayers.
My father takes pictures.
Sometimes my mother smiles
with me for the pictures.
We ride past strawberry fields.
I love to crush ripe strawberries
on my Polish cousins' bare backs
when they work in the fields.

My mother may still be mad
about Warsaw. In the hotel room
I turned on the radio full blast
and pretended to play a guitar.
When my father rushed in to make me
turn it down, I jumped on the bed
and shouted, *nigger music!*
My father flew at me and slapped
me hard in the face. *Don't ever*
say that word again. My ears were hot
and I thought I would burst.
He was always complaining
about nigger music.

My mother isn't smiling
when we arrive at the camp.
I'd apologize if I knew
she were mad at me.
No one looks at me.

There were wooden chairs
with arms but no seats. We see
rugs made from peoples' hair.
It doesn't hurt to get your hair cut.
There was a ton of it in that room.

My mother won't smile at me.
I want to tell her that we are Catholics
and could never be in this kind of trouble.
These people were Jews.
We're Americans, even Dad now.
The guides here say that the Nazis
were the meanest people in the world,
but my Uncle Edek said that
the Russians were the real pigs.
My grandfather said that Hitler
should have killed more Jews.

We go to a room
with two small box cars
on tracks that stop
at two oven doors in a brick wall.
This doesn't make sense.
How could they keep people
in these cars and dump them in an oven?
The people would just jump out.
Someone talks about how the showers
were another way to kill
people. Did they burn them
with hot water?

As we leave the building
this Polish lady runs out,
makes the sign of the cross
with one hand, squeezes
her babushka at her neck
with the other hand and cries,
Matko Boska, Matko Boska,
Mother of God.

Beauty Shop

In order for my father to work in our beauty shop he had to go to cosmetology school and earn a license. My mom had always run her own beauty shops. My father required that the beauty operators (aka the Girls) in our shop call him "Mr. Lucian." He insisted that my mother lead by example in this, as the most senior Girl. The beauty shop was attached to our house. My parents installed a secret two-way mirror in our kitchen and covered it with draperies so they could observe the Girls. When my parents were together the shop was called *Lucian's Hairstyling*, then *Helen's* after their divorce. Later when she sold it, the shop would be renamed *The Miracle on 54th Street.*

The first modern-day miracles I witnessed were in Pittsburgh's First Presbyterian Church in the mid-1970's. The chartered bus from Cleveland left in the dark morning to arrive at the Pittsburgh healing service by 9 a.m. Sleepy pilgrims in the bus shared thermoses of coffee. To get more punch for their prayers, some abstained from food, emitting a putrid fasting halitosis. Upon arrival with my parents at the church, wheelchairs of the faithful already lined the aisles and altar, and a field of crutches jutted above the pews. The air was expectant, joyous in contrast to the somber stained glass windows of Jesus sweating blood in the Garden of Gethsemane and His final walk bearing the cross along the Via Dolorosa.

The preacher was Kathryn Kuhlmann, in a white, flowing gown, the vision of a tall angel with Betadyne red hair. Her voice was the beguiling contralto breeze of the Holy Spirit. Charles Beebe at the organ provided Miss Kuhlmann with an enigmatic background accompaniment of chromatically descending chords. The word *Jesus* could take several seconds. She would interrupt her prayer, pivoting sharply toward the lower balcony, shouting and pointing. *On my left in the balcony: take OUT your hearing aid. YOU, the woman in red, can you hear me NOW? CLAIM your healing. HEAR the Word of God which says 'This is the work of my beloved Son in Whom I am well PLEASED.' Say this after me, "I believe in miracles because I believe in GOD.*" The important words took a full three seconds. All others were delivered gunshot staccato. I thought that if I concentrated hard enough, I could claim the healing of my near-sightedness and present my glasses at the altar to Miss Kuhlmann.

My parents and I attended Miss Kuhlmann's Sunday services at Stambaugh Auditorium in Youngstown, Ohio. We were usually quiet in the car for the hour-long drive because at least two of the three of us were angry. We'd stop for gas first and find the Moody Bible Institute's Sunday radio program. Occasionally there were healings at these Sunday services, but not as often as in Pittsburgh. The Youngstown group was her home flock. The choir, over one hundred strong, dressed formally. The women wore chaste pastel floor-length gowns in rows like butter mints. The choir director was Dr. Metcalfe whose many daughters stood in the front row, each one as tiny and pretty as the next. One was named Pitter for the pitter patter her feet made on the floor. Dr. Metcalfe's handsome profile, white locks and British accent gave a cosmopolitan air to his direction. The portly, grinning gap-toothed assistant minister, called Young David (Verzilli) would officiate if Miss Kuhlmann were out of town conducting healing or revival meetings. His wife, Kathleen, an enhanced Mennonite, was one of the pianists.

Jimmy Miller, the main pianist, kept himself stone solemn despite the surrounding faithful shouting in tongues or being slain in the Spirit. He'd repeat endless refrains of mesmerizing simple hymns about being washed in the Blood of the Lamb,

Marching to Zion, Standing on the Promises, walking and talking In the Garden with Jesus.

The end of the service was signaled by a repetitive *Allelujah,* which reorganized the same three chords for twenty minutes at a time. It could have been divine peace washing over us, but I now realize that it was probably the numbness induced by musical pabulum.

Kathryn Kuhlmann Choir membership entailed Wednesday evening trips to a school gym in Warrensburg close to Youngstown. I took the 52B bus from our house in Parma, Ohio to catch my ride with Margo, a 50 year old woman from Germany who worked in a factory. She ate apples whole, including the core. She drove to Shaker Heights to pick up the rest of our carpool group of six. There was Jerry, who married into a hand-crafted candy family that had a store on Shaker Square. She smelled minty and sweet. We met Sarah, also a fifteen-year-old girl, who was engaged to a thirty-year-old minister. I envied how clear her life course seemed. She could plan her wedding and it would come true. She was beautifully coiffed and made up. She was happy and lovely, and spoke of her future confidently. Her fiancé looked like an Osmond brother. She asked me about the callus on my neck and I told her that it was from playing the violin. She frowned and said, "I could never do anything that would wreck my face."

We Cleveland carpool girls called ourselves the Sunshine Girls and sang at Young David's Friday services at the Old Stone Church on the Square in downtown Cleveland. We sang in unison, a cappella. I was trained enough as a musician to know that this made the texture far too transparent for untrained, inaccurate voices like ours. I felt embarrassed by our singing, but it seemed to bring the congregation some pleasure.

At about the time I joined Miss Kuhlmann's choir, my father was asked to be a Sunday usher. Ushers would pass the basket during services, an interdenominational skill. Ushers also would surround Miss Kuhlmann when the Spirit moved her to walk among her flock. There was the danger that the press of the crowd could hurt her, so the ushers would take positions around her person, bodyguard style.

Miss Kuhlmann commonly engaged in the laying on of hands. She touched my forehead one Sunday along with others' in the choir, and we fell backward one by one, a fallen battalion of Christ. Sometimes the folding wooden chairs would collapse, too. This was called being *slain in the Spirit*.

The organist, Charles Beebe, would rip out majestic, ecstatic arpeggiated chords and suspensions under his speedy hands, practically blurred, all the stops pulled, and you could feel the boom in your chest through the floor, and you knew it was the stirring of the Spirit.

It angered my father that I was reluctant to play hymns on my violin in church services. He said that I wasn't giving God the glory since I only played music written by non-Christians like Beethoven, Brahms, and Bach. Even though Bach ostensibly wrote a lot of music "for the glory of God," there was no record of his being born again. The Devil is clever and often disguises himself in great beauty to trick us into not glorifying God, thereby distracting us from bringing in more souls. At fifteen I began studying the violin with Daniel Majeske, the concertmaster of the Cleveland Orchestra. In his home studio were books written by the evangelist, Billy Graham. One lesson, I dared confess my dilemma of what to play in church, and was secretly hopeful for the potential added benefit of revealing my specialness as a born-again Christian. After his delight about my knowledge of Billy Graham's work, he said, "Oh, playing in church is not a big deal. Just choose a hymn from a hymnal. Play it once through. Then take it an octave above on the repeat. Use the printed key so the organist is not challenged. People love it." This was useful advice from a born-again Christian who played classical music for a living, apparently without guilt.

Mr. Majeske still has the power, after thirty-five years and beyond death, to induce a swarm of icy butterflies in my bowel whenever I drive by the Cleveland Music School Settlement. I had heard that he didn't like teaching girls because they grew up to marry and have kids. Nights before lessons were sleepless, and afternoons afterward I was catatonic. By evening I'd begin to worry about the next lesson. He seemed to need to assert dominance, even though I'd have done anything for him. I'd have promised him my firstborn child, not to mention my virginity or what I understood of it. The five hours of daily violin practice were not a problem.

Terror of Lu paled in comparison to my terror of Mr. Majeske, which was pure, devoid of disdain and hatred. My father must have sensed his own relative lack of power over me. He sulked and complained about how I could admire a total stranger, but not him.

Lu sat with my mom and me at the dinner table but we no longer spoke to him. It was close to the end of his forty-day fast. He wore a pained expression, like that of Christ on the cross. He sat shirtless, grimy from mowing the lawn. Rivulets of dried sweat formed patterns on his chest, further suggesting Christ at his crucifixion.

He read aloud to us from his Pilgrim Edition of the King James Bible. If he needed to scratch his back he would use a dinner fork, not skipping one jot or iota of the Word. The wave of his stench had a singular quality, the fetid smell of an empty, dry stomach. Only evil could produce this stink, as if it billowed from the rank mouth of hell. Maybe it was the breath of his sins escaping his repentant body. It was a good thing that I had attended Girl Scout camp where I learned that if you breathed through your mouth in the latrines, you wouldn't smell anything. I did this while eating soup at the dinner table, its lack of taste a glad price.

I hid a set of silverware for myself in the back of the flatware drawer so that I would never have to use a fork that touched his skin or mouth. I held my breath if I had to pass him in a room.

My mother needed a strategy to divorce my father. She was sure that the law would favor Lu as the abandoned spouse, and that her assets were endangered since the shop was in his name. I tried to influence her by overdosing on aspirin and Sudafed: *just leave him, no matter the consequences.* After a night in the ER I began hypnosis therapy with a Christian therapist who also encouraged my mom to leave him.

While she waited for the right time to file for divorce, we lived with him in silence. He was laid off from his factory work, and he proved not to be a talented beautician. She hated the idea of supporting him so she hid our food from him. If hungry, I'd collect the garage key from her, enter the garage, find the kill switch on the car, unlock it, and find whatever food she had stored in a cooler in the backseat. It was important to replenish the ice so the food wouldn't spoil. Then in reverse order, the car lock, the kill switch, garage lock, key returned.

She was not going to share anything with him. The hiding place for the newspaper was the clothes hamper. The butter was in the mailbox in the colder months. At Christmas he placed some presents beneath a Christmas tree she and I put up, so she moved the tree to another room and left his presents in the middle of the room. When he placed them under the tree in its new location, she moved the tree again. She enjoyed this game and laughed about it to friends. I think she thought she was outsmarting him.

Every day my father placed a bag of Spicettes candy in a kitchen drawer. Every day I ate them all, and he replenished them. I worried that it made him feel as if he were providing for me in a special, secret way while I hoped that it made him angry.

The fun part was leaving no trace. My father listened to cassette tapes of weekly sermons by Kathryn Kuhlman, her assistant, David Verzilli, Billy Graham, or any of the chosen of the evangelical luminati.

These saints provided the soundtrack of my middle childhood. Bible verses more spitted than spoken. Prayers more whiny than pious. My mother and I didn't speak to my father, but the spoken word violated every small room in our small house. My father could easily feel righteous about flooding our airspace: the Lord commanded Christians to *go ye into all the world, and preach the gospel to every creature.* Mark 16:15. Maybe Lu hoped to annoy the hell right out of us in the kitchen.

Cutting up the cassette tapes would be too obvious, and would trigger my father's Job complex, a tiresome habit of thanking God for testing his faith through adversity. *For whom the Lord loveth he chasteneth*. **Hebrews 12:6.** Whenever I'd sniff defiantly, he'd close his eyes and mutter, *Thank you, Jesus.* This took all the fun out of revenge, but fueled it, too.

First I cut the cord off his cassette player. I listened with my ear to my bedroom floor as he reported this to a friend on the phone. He didn't use my name. He said what "they" did to his cassette tape player. "They" as in the Old Testament "enemies" that the psalmist complained to God about in **Psalm 38**, *mine enemies are lively, and they are strong.*

A couple of days later he replaced the cord with a new one and resumed his duty to spread the gospel in our house. Not to be outdone, I submerged the cassette player in a tub of water the next time he was at church, an all day affair which left time for the tape player to appear dry.

Soon I heard the familiar cadences and my heart sank. He had simply bought a new cassette player. I phoned my brother Billy, my adviser in all things illegal and/or scientific. He was eight years my senior and lived on his own. As a child he loved to blindfold me and feed me medicines in the bathroom.

Billy was fascinated with chemistry and magnets. He told me that I could erase an audiotape by magnetizing it. I knew we had a giant magnet in the house, and found it in my father's printing machine toolbox.

The next time he left for church I took the five-pound magnet and glided it in a slow benediction over his entire sermon collection. A chill thrilled me as I effortlessly destroyed his treasure without a trace. We enjoyed at least a few days of silence before he began to buy new sermon tapes.

I ignored my mother's disapproving "Now, what have you accomplished by this, really?" I loved the rush of revenge and when it wore off, I wanted more. I thought I'd prevent him from going to church. I called Billy again. Even though he could teach me how to slash Lu's tires, he advised against it since the destruction of property could get me into trouble, even as a juvenile. It turned out that Billy had a better and less illegal plan.

I waited until Saturday night to unlock the garage door secretly. I perched at the bathroom window to watch, as agreed, for Billy to enter the garage, release the air from Lu's tires, and leave. I then let myself into the garage bringing some string firecrackers Billy had given me, and tied them up to the garage entrances. Muffling my excited chortling I waited and watched at the bathroom window for Lu to emerge from the house at 6 a.m. to drive to church. As he opened the garage door, he leapt back, startled by the sparks. After a moment he proceeded inside to the car but then sprinted back into the house. I put my ear to my bedroom floor to hear him call his friend to wail, "They slashed my tires to keep me from church. Praise Jesus!"

ARCS

Unbeknownst to You, My Brother

Downtown the coroner speaks
with averted eyes about the bullet
and its path from your hand to your head.
He whispers his request
to kindly remove my child from the room.

For your funeral your wife dresses
in plastic shoes and a tight ruby dress.
You don't know that she will never give
our mother your ashes in the cardboard box.
She will scatter them, to your son's horror.

You don't know that one morning
our mother will be found
lying in a field in the muddiness
of her stroke.

Your young son sits in the back row
during the service at the funeral home.
You don't know that he too will die
at your age.

In my Bible
there is no holy card for your funeral
but I have saved a yellow lined
memo sheet from the coroner
with the heading *William J. Brown.*
In my handwriting is
One spent, 5 extra
Smith and Wesson
The coroner, Dr. Edelstein, wrote
S & W Revolver
357 Magnum
Ser# S-305856

The minister glanced down to his notes
during the final prayer
to remind himself of your name.

Luck Runs in My Family

In Poland
during World War II
a certain Nazi
liked to stand my father
against a wall,
walk back,
and fire
his pistol
as close as possible
to my father's head
for sport.
My father didn't
feel lucky,
frozen against the wall,
but he'd live
to call it luck.

My brother Billy
died by shooting
himself. He didn't
know that luck
has nothing to do
with Russian Roulette.

I am lucky
that my daughter is
lucky to be
recovering.
When she burst
into the house
with her eighteen
month medallion
I felt lucky.
I didn't feel lucky
driving her
to those first

counseling meetings.
Her scabbed arms,
shaved head,
and scaly warts
made me look away
as if she were a snail
being torn
from its shell.

Life Expectancy

My father became a death-row chaplain.
During his visits the prisoners' legs
are chained to a large bolt in the floor.
Their hands are bound to their belts.
Mostly they want to talk.

My husband saw a bat
dive headlong into his hardwood floor,
still wet with polyurethane.
The bat struggled to rip away and reclaim its wings.
It was a kindness to chop off its head.

Most death row inmates prefer a life
sentence of God's words, even stories
of the Last Supper and Judgment Day.
A few prisoners would choose a silent ax,
preferring not to be bound with words
to time, like nerves to muscle.

Some prisoners would believe
my father's words about eternal life.
In these inmates' eyes does he recognize
those of his own trespassers.

He reminds himself again
that Christ died for the Nazis, too,
who made him a slave at age 14.
He is bathed in the light
of the caged fluorescent bulbs.

Lucian Wept

For the execution of Harry Mitts
the solemn death house staff
welcomed Lucian inside
from the dark morning
night drive from Cleveland.
Holding hands to pray
with Harry Mitts on the morning
of Mitts' execution was a milestone.
Lucian felt honored.

Mitts was beatific.
For twenty years Lucian visited Mitts
on death row, where he introduced him
to Christ. They exchanged letters.
Mitts sent a photo of himself
with his young smiling daughter
behind the orange bars of a jungle gym
the year before the murders.
Mitts had drawn a smiley face
on the back next to his comment
on the irony of the playground bars.

Many protesters had gathered outside.
Lucian alone was allowed
to accompany Mitts until the last door.
In the observation theater
on the other side of the aisle
the other witnesses with the victims'
families tightened hands
as Mitts in the death chamber
was guided to the stretcher and lay down.
He said his final words.

As an attendant pulled the curtain
across the one-way mirror
to the observation theater, Mitts

extended his hand toward Lucian
as if to say "God bless you" or "thank you."
The closed-circuit monitor displayed
Mitts' face as he received the injection.
His eyes fluttered and closed.
It was the most beautiful death
Lucian had ever envied.

Unbroken Circle

At sixteen I'd had enough.
I left home and my father's life.
For twenty-eight years
I did not miss him once.

After my parents' divorce
we kept him ever-present,
reciting a growing litany of his sins
like a broken rosary.

I searched for solace
in understanding my life's
occurrences, some ordinary,
others blessedly rare:

marriage, but to a man
46 years my senior
who joked sweetly that he didn't know
whether to marry or adopt me;

motherhood, but ten days
after my husband died;
other deaths, divorce;
betrayals, severe depressions;

extreme treatments;
suicide of my brother;
success as a violin teacher;
a child's drug addiction.

In mid-life I crafted a loving family
with the right man. The price extracted
for our joy was ten years of angry,
begrudging silence from my mom and sister.

Through their corrupted lenses

my new husband resembled Lu.
They grieved my love for him
as if it were their loss of me.

My fury from this betrayal
was the only force explosive enough
to blast open my silence with Lu
and the door beyond.

Lu as the bad guy was our dogma.
When they excised me from their lives,
they cleaved this family foundation
and cleared way for a new frame.

Lucian would not have recognized me, his daughter, even if he were not suffering from early Alzheimer's. It had been twenty-eight years since we had seen each other. At the appointed time he stood in the Cleveland Sheraton hotel lobby stock-still, his raincoat folded over his arm. He was dressed as I remembered him: suit, dress shoes, spit and polish, Brylcreem with middle notes of Mennen aftershave.

I introduced myself, my husband, and two grown daughters. There were his jokes and complaints about the hotel buffet, after giving thanks for it in Jesus' name in a Scottish/Polish accent. After decades of revising the family mythologies, there was little to say that could connect us. I was about to learn that the information that mattered had been missing and came from a world before my own beginnings, from his life as a boy in Nazi-occupied Poland and Germany.

In his 83rd year, my father lost the last of his siblings in Poland, his sister, Kamila. She often spoke of jumping with him on their bed as children. The two of them also shared Alzheimer's disease. He wanted to go to Poland for the funeral.

A Cleveland friend drove him to his Chicago flight while arguing for six hours about whether there was a direct flight from Cleveland to Warsaw. He would forget that the matter was settled. Then his complaint about the Chicago traffic would trigger his certainty about a direct flight, thus opening the loop again.

He admired all of his nieces and nephews who took excellent care of his sister, so selflessly. They did their duty without complaint. They wouldn't even think of putting her in a home. When her Alzheimer's was less pronounced, he'd accused them of babying her. She was just looking for attention, he said.

For his return trip a car service worker made a sign with his name in large letters and walked him to his last connection. He repeated his prayers. He would need to trust God about his great fear, that the car service driver wouldn't recognize him.

On the plane in coach he sat squarely. His full head of barely grey hair was neatly combed and slicked down. His only concession to comfort was loosening the laces of his patent leather shoes. He wore a no-iron collared shirt. In his jacket pocket was a clean handkerchief and pocket-sized New Testament, the red-letter edition, which highlights the words of Christ. His lapel pin was a double flag, the U.S.A. and Poland. He was amazed to be served three meals in the course of one flight. He watched the clouds from his window and thought of the loving arms of Christ. In his wallet he carried his red glossy business cards with an extended hand drawn under the words *Reach Out Ministries* and a reference to his favorite Bible quote:

For God so loved the world that he gave his only begotten Son, that whosoever believeth in Him should not perish, but have everlasting life. John 3:16.

For Any Abiding Place on Earth

after Carl Dennis

All my grandmother needed at her farm in Poland
was time to raise the crops of corn and cousins.

I met my grandmother when I was seven.
As our taxi from Warsaw came to a stop in the dust
she sputtered and screamed around this barnyard
with the alarmed chickens. She tugged off her apron
and tucked her hair into her babushka.

I stand at the farm's grave and find only ceramic tile pieces
in the disemboweled earth where the kitchen once stood.

There are no abiding places on earth, unless memory is a place
and I doubt it. Gather all memories and they wouldn't fill
one square inch of this remembered ground.
They are lighter than dust and even less confined.

Originals of comments excerpted on the back cover:

In Lucia May's inaugural poetry collection, *Blond Boy,* she records with gracious precision the personal horrors of the boy who would become her father. Taken from his home by the Nazis, the boy's humanity was forever scarred by his experiences. Of his torture, Lucia writes, "...the boys accepted their penalties/like cows on the farm before the knife." Lucia weaves his story into her own through poetry that is brutally honest while being "bathed in the light" of forgiveness. She manages well the difficult task of showing grief and loss unsentimentally, with a glance, a gesture, an image that glows vividly on the page. This slim book offers readers the chance to share in emotions as complex as Bach played with panache on a well-tuned violin. At the end, we are left with memories that are "lighter than dust and even less confined."

—Linda Back McKay, author of *The Next Best Thing* and *Out of the Shadows: Stories of Adoption and Reunion*.

A man who suffered a wretched childhood extended bitterness and perverse misery to his own children. He became a religious fanatic, who in his distorted view deemed the music of Bach and Beethoven wholly unacceptable. Growing up in a nightmarish environment, his daughter, Lucia P. May, did not fall victim to depression, suicide, alcoholism or drug addiction. Miss May escaped the quicksand of her father's cruelty through art, music and literature. She writes exquisite poetry that shines light in the darkness.

—Robert O Fisch, author of *Light from the Yellow Star: A Lesson of Love from the Holocaust* and *The Sky Is Not the Limit*

Lucia Piaskowiak May writes without any sentimentality whatsoever about her father's life in World War II Poland and about the shadow he cast over her own life. She compresses enormous emotion into tense spare lines to create poetry that is fierce and true.

—Keith Maillard, author of *The Clarinet Polka*

A memoir in poetry, in *Blond Boy* Lucia May tells the tragic and amazing story of her father's survival in Nazi-occupied Poland, his marriage to her mother, her visit to Auschwitz, taking violin lessons and attending healing services at a Presbyterian church. This is a story well worth telling and it comes wonderfully alive in all its mesmerizing details. These memories will dance in our minds for a long time. May writes of them as 'lighter than dust and even less confined.' May we all be thankful that she has captured them for a moment.

—Mary Logue, author of *Hand Work* and *Trees*

Lucia May's book, *Blond Boy*, is a tough, intense collection of poems. It's a book about what luck means. It's a book about a father, that blond boy who survived World War II, and where the luck of surviving led him. It's a collection that offers its readers portraits of a family, of how religion affected them, vignettes that allow us to see a family's suffering, and how pain and discord shaped their lives. We are given stories that cover many years, and we see how the lucky and unlucky in this single family lose or find their strength, their sense of purpose inside a family, inside history. This collection is blunt in its truth-telling, and ambitious in its range. I won't forget these poems.

—Deborah Keenan, author of *From Tiger to Prayer* and *so she had the world*